Hiker's Guide For Beginners:
Meal Planning and Wilderness Cooking to Long Distance

Table of Contents

Introduction

Welcome to a Hiker's Guide to Meal Planning and Wilderness Cooking, a DIY guide that is meant to help you plan out your meals to get the nutrients you need to make the most of a hike. Many people pack unnecessary foods or foods that will weigh them down, use tools that they really don't need and have to replace every time they're out on a hike, but this guide is meant to help mitigate some of those issues so that you can try to get the most out of your hike. Whether you're hiking for a couple days, wanting to hike but can't for fear of losing weight, or hiking for a day, this book has a little something of everything to help you out. Let's begin.

Chapter 1 – Basing Your Diet on Your Hike

It's very important to realize that most of your dieting affects how you hike, both at the beginning of the hike and at the end of the hike. The reason for this is because it is your body's prerogative to digest and use energy as soon as it is available rather than using stores of your energy. Therefore, you need to determine your reasons for taking a hike because if you are taking a hike in order to lose weight then you do not want to pack a lot of food, but if you are taking the hike to just hike then you will want to pack an increased amount of food as you will burn more calories than if you were just taking a walk.

3 or 5 breaks

Regardless of what type of hike you're doing, you want to take periodical breaks because you could either be using up too much energy at one time and you don't have enough calories or fat to burn it off or your muscles are simply too strained in order to continue further. The 3 to 5 rule is really based on your preference because you can either take 3 breaks of 20 minutes or you can take 5 breaks of 10 minutes and this depends on how fit you are. For instance, since I weigh somewhere around 320 pounds I would want to take 5 breaks of 10 minutes because while I want my body to temporarily rest, I know that I am too overweight to get back into the motion once I stop for long enough periods. However a person who is trying to increase their muscle density and is already in good shape, would want to take a break of 20 minutes 3 times as this allows the muscles to take a prolonged break during an intense exercise and forces them to rip and repair more than if they were to let the muscle only partially relax. This is why the three or five rule depends on your weight, but it is really effective if you are trying to use hiking as an exercise tool.

Understanding nutrition

Understanding your nutrition is absolutely vital for having a good hike because you cannot have a good hike if you're malnourished. A case example that explains this really well is dehydration, which is an extreme case, but does allow for a good example. During dehydration, you are dealing with a lack of water in your diet and it affects your perception as well as how much work you're actually doing on your body. In the same way, understanding that without calories you cannot have energy is going to be absolutely vital when you're about to use a lot of energy.

Calories

Calories are the pinnacle of pretty much every single nutrition diet manual on the planet. The reason is actually really good because without calories you don't have energy, even when you're burning fat you're still burning calories. You don't lose weight by burning energy you lose weight by burning calories which produce energy and these calories are held inside of that. That isn't to be confused with the fat that you find in food, because the fat on your body is much different than fat found in food because the fat in your body is already made to be burned into energy while the fat in food is currently in the raw form and has to be transformed into the ready-made fat that we have in our bodies.

Carbohydrates

Carbohydrates are one of two parts that you need in order to increase your muscle density. You primarily want soluble fiber and a little bit of insoluble fiber rather than any sugar at all. So low fiber means that it's fiber that can be digested and incorporated via water, while insoluble is the one that makes you go poop all the time because you can't dissolve it inside of water. Sugar is your absolute enemy when it comes to using energy because it provides a small boost of energy but also creates a deficiency in some of your inner workings, like the insulin process that makes it harder to burn more energy after you've used the energy from the sugar.

Protein

Protein is the second part of the muscle building process because while carbohydrates serve as the building material for making muscle, protein serves as the nutrient mechanism that uses the building material. You need a lot of water and protein in order for protein to use the carbohydrates to build your muscle. You primarily get carbs from plants and protein from meat.

Fats

Fat is often misconstrued as always being bad, but the truth is that some of them are healthy. Saturated fat and trans fat are chemically built to be complex, which makes them difficult for the body to break down. We just can't break them down as fast as we can other fats. The healthy fats are the polyunsaturated fat and monounsaturated fat, which are simple fats that we can break down very easily and get out of the body. Trans fat happens to be the worst and is actually banned in some countries.

Sodium

Sodium is also given a bad name but you actually need it to have water retention inside of your body. You just have to think of the salt and sand bags that are used for water emergencies to realize that you need salt in order to hold water inside of your body. Therefore, if you don't have enough salt inside of your body you can actually die from dehydration. The recommended maximum amount of sodium inside of your body is 2,500 milligrams provided by the FDA, but you should have more than 1,000 milligrams of sodium a day if you're on a diet (or more, not less).

Potassium

We need something that actually uses the water in our bodies and puts it to use, which is where potassium comes from. The reason why most doctors and health advisors tell you that you need more potassium in your diet if you have cramps is because potassium is the thing that you need in order to use the water that you put inside your body. If you don't have enough potassium in your body then your body just will not use the water effectively. You need around 4,400 mg of potassium on a regular basis, so I suspect you need a lot more for when you go on an intensive hike.

Chapter 2 – How to decrease calorie burn

Sometimes we don't actually want to burn a lot of calories while we're hiking because we're just hiking so that we can enjoy it. That isn't to say that we are always going to use hiking as a period of enjoyment, but there are some of us who don't want to go underneath a specific amount of weight and they need to watch how many calories they burn. The problem with this is that you can't really go outside and enjoy yourself if you're trying to keep weight or even gain weight. Some people really dislike this because it removes a lot of their good habits out of their daily activities like hiking, which means that you need to find ways in order to prevent you from burning a lot of calories while you're out enjoying your activity. This section is dedicated to those people.

Decrease Body Temperature

One of the aspects that isn't really covered, when people begin to lose weight, is their body temperature because as your body temperature goes up you begin to burn more calories. This isn't really covered because if you're exercising then your body temperature normally goes up by itself and this is the point of exercising. Your internal body temperature isn't actually going up because your body has a bunch of mechanisms that keep it in a relative range of temperatures and you are sweating so that you can cool down your body so that it maintains an exact body temperature. This is what I mean by "you need to decrease your body temperature when you are exercising via a hike."

There are a few things that you can do to lower your body temperature, which means you can prevent your body temperature from burning calories as much as it would normally if you were to be hiking for exercise. The first thing that you can do is you can use shaded areas while you're hiking because most of the body heat that you're going to be generating comes from your body and from the sun that's beating down on your back. The sun naturally brings your body's water and liquid to a boiling point, which is why your body has specific measures put in place in order to prevent you from going over. By using shaded areas, you are naturally avoiding the rays of the sun that boil the liquids in your body.

Another way that you can potentially limit the amount of calories that you burn is by simply standing in front of the wind. The beauty about sweating is that you are priming yourself to a situation where the wind can cool your body down much faster because you are already wet and water cools down at a rapid pace. Normally, this is called a wind chill effect and it's actually used when describing the weather in the outside world by weathermen. By standing still and allowing the wind to brush against your skin, you naturally lower your body's temperature.

Another part that you can do to lower your body temperature is to simply stop moving and what I mean by this is that you will want to take breaks repeatedly as you're traveling up the hill. If you notice yourself sweating, then it's usually a good time to stop hiking because your body has gotten to the point where the internal body temperature is no longer being maintained by normal body functions. It means that your body has been pushed past the limit of sedentary, which means you've been push passed the point of not doing anything that requires intensive activity. By taking a small break over an extended period of time, you will allow your body the ability to slowly bring down the temperature to the point where it can stabilize and continue at that temperature for a further amount of time.

Path of Least Resistance

One of the best solutions to not burning as many calories as you would normally is to simply take the path of least resistance and this refers to how some hikes have large inclines that you have to climb up. However, there are options for you to go around in order to go up to that specific height. Most people tend to want to take the most direct route and this includes taking the climbing adventure that everyone loves about hiking. You burn significantly more calories by climbing up a 90 degree angle, but you do not burn more if the incline is less than that. The path of least resistance provides you with a way to consistently avoid things that continuously put pressure on your muscles, which raise your body temperature. Additionally, by taking the path of least resistance you also prevent the need for your muscles to work harder to achieve the same result. This means you burn even less calories from your muscles not needing to do as much work and you also burn less calories from not raising your body temperature.

More Horizontal Less Vertical

Another reason why you might be burning calories is if you're going in a vertical direction rather than a horizontal direction. This is the same principle behind the path of least resistance, but it allows you to choose hikes that are appropriate for you. For instance, when you're on a hike and in a forest area you may find that your hike includes going up over a hill or many hills because of how the hike is laid out. However, there are several other hikes that are not as intensive as that and you want to select the height that is more horizontal because it allows you to take a straight path that doesn't increase the work put on your calves to support the amount of work that would require you fighting against gravity.

Chapter 3 – Making Your Meals

One of the most important things that you can do before you actually go on a hike is to prepare your food. There are plenty of guys out there that will tell you how to catch fish or how to notice the plants around you, but this guy is going to tell you how to actually plan out meals that you make at home. Most of us will usually carry around a backpack that's full of pre-made food, maybe a sleeping bag, along with a bunch of different useful advice that will help us in specific areas of our hike. Therefore, this section will help you pack what you need in your food for your height.

High Protein and High Carbs

We've already talked about the importance of high protein and high carbs, because carbs are the raw material that allow you to build muscle while protein is the one that actually builds it for you. For this very reason you need to calculate how much protein and carbohydrates that you are putting inside of your body, which is what this section is here for . To calculate for protein is extremely easy because all you have to do is take your weight and divide it by 2.2, which will give you an estimated amount of what your weight should be for your height. Therefore, if you weigh around 300 pounds and you divided that by 2.2 then you would come out with an estimate of 136 grams of protein. Carbohydrates on the other hand tend to get a bad rap because of the famous Atkins diet and the proof that if you eat less carbohydrates throughout the day then you will lose a ton of weight. The problem with that is that yes, you will lose a lot of weight but it will also be in the form of your own muscle. You should have around 100 to 150 grams in total for the day if you're not doing anything too drastic. If you are hiking on the other hand, then you should probably have closer to 200 grams of carbohydrates in a single day. This means that for almost every gram of protein that you have you should have 2 grams of carbohydrates. For instance, if you have a weight of 176 then you want around 80 grams of protein while also taking in around a 160 grams of carbohydrates. This allows the body to utilize those carbohydrates with the protein to increase muscle production while on your hike. However, you don't want to do all of this in one sitting because then your body will reject it because it cannot absorb that much nutrition in one go. If you try to do it, then you would likely end up either having diarrhea or constipation.

A good example of something that would mix these two highly concentrated necessities would be an egg sandwich because eggs are exceedingly high in protein by being around 6 to 9 grams of protein inside of each egg, while bread is usually really good at being high in carbs and mayo is really good at being high in protein and carbs as well. Obviously, you would want to select the one with lower fat but you could easily eat two of these sandwiches and have 30% of your daily needs met. We all have different preferences, so knowing that you should have high protein and high carbs inside of your meal before you head out to a high-energy activity is a good start to planning out which food you want to include.

Small Fats

Even though fats tend to get really bad names from the diet and health industry, they also regulate your mood. If you've ever wondered why people who eat salads and those who tend to avoid fats tire easily and are usually those who are more prone to look up self-help books on depression, or similar topics, then you will realize that it's because of the lack of fat. That's not to say that a fat-free diet is bad, it just affects your mood in a negative way because fats help keep you happy. Fats are the things that lubricate the fatty areas of your body. Therefore, having a small amount of healthy fat is really good for you but you only want a small amount because even if it's the healthy fat you don't want much of it inside of your body. You just want enough to improve the lubrication and your body to keep down the irritation that an exercise will have on your body.

High Potassium and Medium Sodium

You need a lot of potassium and a lot of people tend to overlook this fact when they keep on suggesting things like low carb diets. You already know the requirements for sodium from the first chapter, so I will go over what you should be looking for in potassium. On an average basis the human body consumes around 2,000 milligrams of sodium, which is nowhere near the amount that you should be eating. Ironically, out of all of the nutrients inside of that nutritional fact, potassium should have the highest number of all of them. It is recommended that you should consume around 4,700 milligrams of potassium on a daily basis. To give you an idea of just how much that is, you only need to eat around 7 - 8 whole potatoes in order to fit that model. The beauty about this is that if you consume around 7 - 8 whole potatoes in order to fit the model, you will have consumed around 14 - 16 grams of dietary fiber while consuming around 21 - 32 grams of your daily need for protein. The best part about potatoes in their raw form is that they don't actually have any sodium. It is the French fry or any fried food dealing with potatoes that cause the issue.

Chapter 4 – Name of the Chapter

Unless you plan on carrying a torch with you the entire time you try to hike up a hill or you plan to carry a starter kit whenever you go out to hike, you may just want to enjoy the fact that you can sit down and make fire without any extra tools from the outside world. A fire like this is very useful and beyond making the tinder and the ignition, most of this section will still be useful to even those who decide to bring along kits to make a fire. That's because we teach you how to make a fire home for your fire, which utilizes the lesser known aspects of a fire.

Making The Tinder

While you can make the tinder beforehand you can also make it in the wild rather easily because trees are dying all the time. There's a special type of wood called puck wood that allows you to light it on fire very quickly and it burns really well. It burns rather slow but it's very quick to light because it's got a dry outside but a rather wet core. The way you can identify puck wood is that it's got a very dry orange look on the outside and it comes from a dead tree that's laying on the ground. Once you get some puck wood, you can usually make your tinder out of it but it's not something that you want to make an entire pile of wood from. If all you have around you is wet wood then puck wood would do what you needed it to do but add piece of wood that is fully dead and isn't our specialty wood and it is going to burn a lot slower than our specialty wood because there's less material to actually burn in the inside that's still mostly flammable. On the inside of a tree, most of the stuff that you can burn is stuff that can transfer heat easily from and completely dead wood does not transfer heat very easily. Anything that has a small amount of water in it will transfer heat very easily. Additionally, our specialty wood is not going to be as common as the completely dead wood.

The puck wood is what you're going to be transferring the fire to but in order to get the fire from a homemade version of making an ignition you want a very different form of tinder before you do the transfer. The most common method of tinder is a piece of cloth but if you can't get a piece of cloth then some dried out leaves will do very well. The idea of the leaf is that it doesn't hold a lot of water because it's already dead and because it's very small. Another option for getting that flame to be bigger and to the point where you can light the wood on fire is using dried out weeds but considering the fact that weeds tend to be more condensed, this should really be a second option because you might run into the fact that they haven't all dehydrated from the last rain at their roots.

Make The Fire Home

To begin making a fire you want to first lay the foundation of the fire and the foundation of fire is actually really small because you want it to light up really quickly. These small sticks will go on the inside while the thicker more log like sticks will go around the outside. You want to make three fourths of a square on the bottom for about an inch so that you can stick the puck wood inside. This area should be around 2 - 3 inches wide of small sticks and the area inside of the square should be around an inch to 2 inches thick or as thick as you need it for the puck wood to get inside. Once those little sticks burn you want the fire to last much longer so you begin to pile up much bigger and thicker logs around it in a more complete square. This allows the fire to light very quickly and be smothered by the wood while also having a running airflow through it, but also allowing it to burn further as it gets bigger and requires more material to burn.

Making The Ignition

If you decided that you didn't want to bring along a lighter or fire kit starter, then this is the perfect section for you because we now need to have a method of ignition for the fire. In order to begin you first need two big blocks of wood, a stick that is very short but thick and can be turned quickly, and a very long stick that's rather bendy. Then you will need a few weeds that you pick up from around the area that you've managed to tie together into a rope. Once you have tied the weeds into a rope you now need to tie them to the long-stick. Once you tie them to the long stick you need to put that little stick in the middle of those weeds and then flip the long-stick over so that the little stick is trapped inside of the weeds and the weeds encircle the little stick. Then you use the two big blocks of wood to horizontally hold the little stick in place vertically. At first you're going to want to move back and forth really slowly until all the weeds are used to the motion of moving back and forth because otherwise you'll break your device and have to build it again. However once you do build it and get it used to the motion, then you can move it back and forth repeatedly until you get a smoke rising from the 2 blocks of wood. This is the most common method of starting a fire out on your own.

Lighting The Fire

Once you have your ignition and you've set your puck wood on fire, you need to handle the next couple of moments very diligently because you can't just stick it inside of the fire home and expect it to absolutely work every single time. Essentially, you want to stick it in there and slowly blow on it so that it builds up to jumping onto the other branches in the area. When you build your fire home, the little square that you built it around should catch on fire depending on how high your fire climbs from your puck wood. While you blow on it, the excess energy caused by your breath by providing both nitrogen and oxygen to the fire will increase the fire to the point where it should be able to light the branches above it just fine. Additionally, during this process you should be feeding the fire with dead branches and leaves so that it can continue to burn until the main fire home lights on fire. Even if the fire home is currently on fire in the beginning, you still want to blow on it and nurse it into a much bigger fire. Once it's in that bigger fire, you don't really need to worry about it and so long as you provide it with food it will usually last throughout the night. if you're not trying to last throughout the night then obviously you don't need to do much more than that and you just need to make sure that you put it out once you're done cooking your stuff.

Chapter 5 – Cooking Meat and Water

While you may not always need to cook meat on your hike, you will probably always need to filter out your water. People who tend to bring along meat or have meat to cook have usually gotten the meat via hunting. The primary meat that you want is fish and there are several reasons why you want fish. In order to understand how to cook meat, you actually have to understand how to filter water the best way possible.

Filtering Water

Filtering water is not that complicated because all you have to do is bring it up to a boil and then let it chill, provided you scoop out the dead parasites that present themselves as a film on top because... that's just gross. Once the water reaches a boil, it's automatically good to drink but you have to let it cool down because it will burn your tongue otherwise. If you are going on a hike that's going to last a couple of days or for an entire day then you will likely want to bring a pot along with you because bringing a pot along makes this a lot easier. Otherwise, you will need to find a very thin rock or a very wet leaf that's big. If you don't want to bring along a pot so that you can boil water you can bring along a metal canister that will not melt in fire and that will work just as well. In fact, the metal canister will be more apt to the filtering process that's the best in comparison to the pot or the leaf. The reason being is that the pot will only boil the water and you won't really have a way to collect the steam from it so you will have to use some additional form of filter to get the dead parasites out of the water that you're using to cook the meat or you're using to drink.

On the other hand, if you use a bottle that is able to withstand the temperatures of the fire you can have a tube and another bottle to collect the steam that comes from that and that water will be crystal clear of parasites and bacteria. The entire purpose is to first filter the water to make it safe for you to drink or for you to cook food with, but either way you want to filter the water of parasites and bacteria and then dump the dead bodies out before you begin cooking or drinking from it. Using the steam method, you don't have to use an additional filter because all of this steam has all of the dead bodies and stuff removed from it. Now the other method of filtering out the water is to take a cloth along with some rocks, some sand, some more rocks, some more sand and then putting that in order in a bottle so that you can pour the boiling water through it and those materials will filter it. This won't really filter it to a point where it's 100% safe, but it will filter it to where it is maybe around 60 to 75% safe.

Boil or Grill

Once you filter the water you can begin boiling the meat inside of it or you can drink it. In this book we're just going to cover fish because fish is what you really should be eating on the adventures and you should stay away from red meat. The reason why you should stay away from red meat is because red meats usually consist of a lot more parasites because they can consume both water parasites as well as land-borne parasites. The fish that you find in the water tend to not have as many land-borne parasites, which is why you should be eating more fish than red meat on your ventures. In order to cook fish, you just need to pay attention to the way the fish meat looks. The first sign that it's cooked is that the fish meat will be white instead of somewhat see through. The second sign is that it will be mostly dry when you touch it and pull it apart. Additionally, if it doesn't pull apart right away and it still wants to stay intact and feels like slime then it's definitely nowhere near done. That's pretty much it in terms of boiling your fish, but it's a little bit different if you decide to use the fire to cook your fish because you can cook your fish inside of leaves that are continuously made wet so that you essentially grill the fish instead. The reason why this is a little bit different is because most of the time you can tell when fish is done in the fire because the meat itself will be charbroiled. It may not have the fancy shmancy cool grill lines on it but it will have a slight tinge of "cooked" on the outside of it. This is because the skin is heated up far faster than the inside of the fish.

Conclusion

Welcome to the end of this book, but this isn't the end of your journey because this nowhere near covers everything that there is to talk about. In fact, I went over the intended amount that I wanted to cover because I just wanted you to have the needed knowledge to move forward from the basic. I want you to very carefully go over the safety recommendations for cooking fish and other types of meat just in case you want to eat those meats on your hike but also don't stop searching for answers because the most valuable tool that you can have out in the wilderness is going to be the knowledge that's inside your head. It's the difference between a person being able to survive in the city but die in the forest and a person being able to survive in both. Until next time, good luck.

FREE Bonus Reminder

If you have not grabbed it yet, please go ahead and download your special bonus report *"DIY Projects. 13 Useful & Easy To Make DIY Projects To Save Money & Improve Your Home!"*

Simply Click the Button Below

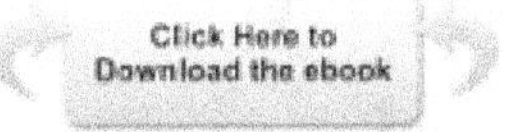

OR **Go to This Page**

http://diyhomecraft.com/free

BONUS #2: More Free & Discounted Books or Products

Do you want to receive more Free/Discounted Books or Products?

We have a mailing list where we send out our new Books or Products when they go free or with a discount on Amazon. Click on the link below to sign up for Free & Discount Book & Product Promotions.

=> Sign Up for Free & Discount Book & Product Promotions <=

OR Go to this URL